Throop Mill and

Throop Mill, situated on the Riv[...]
its last miller Cecil Biles (known t[...]
at the mill. Cis, who loved the mill, worked in it for [...]r
part of his life. Since the time of his death this Grade II listed mill
has been empty and recently calls have been made for an
investigation into the state of the building amid fears that as a
result of its deterioration Bournemouth will lose a picturesque and
key part of the local area's industrial heritage. The mill is situated
in the Throop and Muccleshell Village Conservation Area. The
present building dates from the late 19th century and contains
some fine early 20th century milling machinery.

Throop Mill

Throop Mill, originally known as Holdenhurst Mill, has always has been an important part of the life of the villages of Holdenhurst and Throop. The mill was mentioned in the Domesday Book but it is thought that there has been a mill on the site since Saxon times.

In the Domesday Survey of 1086 the mill was valued at fifteen shillings for tax purposes. The survey also stated that there was a chapel and three fisheries serving the manor hall at Holdenhurst known then as Holeest from the old English for 'wooded hill where holly grows'. In Saxon times, during the reign of Edward the Confessor, the manor was owned by Earl Tostig who died of his injuries received during the Battle of Stamford Bridge. After the Norman Conquest, William I gave the manor to Hugh de Port, a Norman baron who had already acquired much land in Wessex. Hugh de Port later granted all rights to the river and mill to the Abbot of Savigny in northwest France.

The manor at Holdenhurst, although large, was subsidiary to the main manor, the Honour of Twynham (later renamed Christchurch), as was the manor belonging to the Church of the Holy Trinity, later to become Christchurch Priory. The Lord of the Honour was the overlord to the lesser manors. From Saxon times, at least as far back as King Alfred, the overlord was the King.

On ascending the throne in 1100, Henry I gave the Honour of Twynham, including the manor at Holdenhurst, to Richard de Redvers, Earl of Devon, his relative, supporter and friend. The Honour remained in the de Redvers family for many generations until Isabel de Fortibus conveyed the manor to King Edward I on her death in 1293.

Quarr Abbey on the Isle of Wight was founded by Baldwin de Redvers, Richard's son, in c.1132 with monks from Savigny, which was near Baldwin's lands in France. The monks from Quarr Abbey worked in the mill at Holdenhurst which they rented from the lord of the manor. The de Redvers appear to have been fair, even generous, feudal lords and granted their tenants and Christchurch Priory many privileges including the right of riverine fishing.

Throop Mill Pool is still popular for fishing

In 1272, when the mill had been assessed for tax purposes at one guinea, Isabel de Fortibus gave all rights of the mill to the monks. Ten years later Christchurch Priory took on the lease of the mill.

By 1321, the value of the mill had dropped to four shillings and Quarr Abbey decided to give away all its rights to the mill. An ancient charter shows that in 1323 King Edward II gave the mill to the Priory of Christchurch.

For centuries the millers were tenants working for their feudal lord and the hamlet of Throop grew up around the mill. At one time it even had its own inn, The Jolly Sailor, which has since been demolished. For many years the village post office was housed in one of the old cob-walled cottages built beside the road that runs through the village. Throop House, further along Throop Road, has a good view of the river and Pigshoot Ford. It was built 200 years ago and was the home of Sylvia, Dowager Countess of Malmsbury. (In 1863 the Earl of Malmesbury bought the Manor of the Borough of Christchurch from the estate of Sir George Henry Rose and the manor remains in the Malmsbury family to this day.)

Throop village with its gas lamps

'Pigshoot' was mentioned in the 1805 Christchurch Award although the name is probably much older than this and refers to the piece of land adjoining the ford. Pigs were taken here and allowed to root, thereby keeping them off the pastures.

Looking across Pigshoot Ford to the Pigshoot

Throughout the ages the fords across the River Stour to Hurn were in constant use, especially by smugglers. There is an account of the occasion in 1780 when Edward Hooper, a magistrate and a Commissioner of Customs, was entertaining Lord Shaftesbury at Hurn Court. Several smugglers' wagons heavily loaded with kegs of spirit passed by at full speed, Hooper resolutely refusing to look out of the window. The smugglers managed to escape capture because the revenue men decided against following them through the tricky crossings of Pigshoot and the Leaden Stour fords. When an officer of dragoons later called at Hurn Court to ask if smugglers had passed Hooper was able to say that he had seen nothing.

At the beginning of the 19th century Throop Mill was owned by Mathew Aldridge the Younger, and in the late 1850s the miller was James Aldridge. In 1878 records show Mrs Martha Aldridge was living in nearby Stour View House, a fine 18th century house.

Stour View House with its fine Georgian porch

At one time this was the home of a maltster and ships' biscuit maker. After the flour had been ground at the mill, the malt was processed in a long, low-lying building adjacent to the house. George Whitcher owned the mill at the time and he employed a Mr Hockey to manage the mill. Mr Whitcher lived at Throop Villa which is no longer in existence but stood opposite the Congregational Church in the village.

In the 1890s the mill was rebuilt. The old cob walls were taken down and replaced by the red brickwork of the current building.

Throop Mill and the mill race

In about 1925 the mill was bought by Mr Parsons who lived in Holdenhurst Road. During his time at the mill he cleaned and renovated the mill race. When it was altered in 1944 ancient foundations, great blocks of stone, were uncovered and old English pennies and Spanish and Portuguese coins were recovered from the mill stream. Mr Parsons was also responsible for erecting garages along the road beside the mill.

The Mill and garages from Throop Road

In 1958 Mr Parsons sold the mill, excluding the water rights, to the current owners Heygate & Sons Ltd. 'Heygates' are an old established company based near Northampton and have been involved in flour milling since the 18th century.

Flour was still ground by water power until the Second World War when a diesel engine was installed to supplement and double the capacity. Rollers eventually replaced the millstones and the last time the millstones were used was at the end of the war when two hundred tons of wholemeal flour was ground to fulfil a government contract to supply the capitulating German troops. Throop Mill was probably unique in the fact that it had not only a complete roller milling plant but also pairs of millstones ready for use.

In 1960 the diesel engine was removed and replaced by an electric motor as a back-up to the turbine when the need arose. The 50 inch turbine was made by the Ringwood firm Armfield Engineering. Even after the rollers were installed water power was produced by the turbine until 1972 when the mill ceased being operational. When the mill was closed down, the wooden hursting, primary gearing and millstones were all removed and used to restore another mill in Northamptonshire, although the turbine was left. The owners then used the premises to store flour, bran and animal feed.

To return to the last miller, Cis Biles, who loved the mill so much his spirit seems to be part of it. Cis was born in Winton in 1899. He served in India and Egypt during the First World War and afterwards ran his own smallholding in Throop. His connection with the mill began in 1929 when he offered his help as they were short staffed. Shortly afterwards he became the full-time miller and spent many happy hours here for the next 52 years, loving every minute of his work and never taking time off, for a holiday or for illness. The mill became part of him and he was always pleased to talk about his work there to those who showed an interest.

Cis did practically everything in the mill, and for the last few years of his life he worked entirely alone. An old cash book of the 1940s shows his neat handwriting, all items methodically detailed. For example, flour was entered at 40 shillings a sack in 1945, much of it sent out to the military establishments in Southampton, Aldershot and Portland. In 1949 W.D. Bakery of Tidworth were paying £134 3s 4d for 50 sacks.

Cis Biles

Cis was strong. Where big, muscular fellows struggled to raise hundredweight sacks of flour, Cis lifted them up easily and threw them over his shoulders as if they were feather pillows. His heart was pure gold: to him black was black and white was white and there was no grey. Punctuality was one of his gods. Every day he rode his bike to work.

River Stour

Every year before 1972 the River Stour overflowed its banks and the fields all around the mill were flooded. The farmers never minded this as the water was rich with silt which did much to benefit their fields. The mill had full control of the hatches and therefore was never flooded.

When the river was diverted in 1972, one of the senior staff of the Wessex Water Authority stated quite firmly, "You'll be free from flooding from now onwards." But Cis replied promptly, "You may be a much brainier man than me, but I've been here all my life and you've interfered with nature and nature will find a way. You say that this area will not flood in the winter but this place will flood sometime between November and January; that I can promise you." That winter there was flooding in Throop as usual and for the first time the ground floor of the mill was flooded too.

His son, Ron Biles, took on the role of water bailiff and caretaker of the mill from his father and had a great affinity with the mill too. When Ron attended the old Holdenhurst School (now demolished) from the age of 5 he remembers visiting his father regularly at the mill.

Cis's last wish was that he should die at the mill was granted. Ron movingly described his father's death which he felt was almost like a premonition. For many years Cis had not been able to reach the top floors of the mill saying that he was much too old to climb the stairs. On his 82nd birthday he said to his neighbour that he'd had a marvellous life, and that he had only one wish left: that he could ride his bike to work and that his sons would carry him out of the mill. Shortly afterwards he climbed to the very top of the mill to paint the window overlooking the road. The paint was found on the floor where he collapsed and died and his sons did indeed carry him out through the mill door. Ron said afterwards that there was no need for him to paint the window as it had recently been done by painters.

At his funeral Cis was taken past his beloved mill and the road was lined with cars and people wishing to pay their respects to him and the little church at Throop was packed for the service.

Public Footpath over the weir

In 1987 Heygates, the owners of the mill, in conjunction with the South East Dorset Fringe Project opened the mill to the public on certain days. This proved to be very popular, especially as a footpath which follows a very pleasant stretch of the River Stour crosses the weir and passes the mill providing an interesting stop en route for many walkers.

This long weir has six sluice gates; three were made by the Dorset Ironfoundry Company of Poole and the others were made by Lott & Walne of Dorchester and inscribed 'Avon Stour Catchment Board, 1936'. Later Friends of Throop Mill took over the arrangements for providing public access to the mill.

Machinery for the sluice gates

Mill water turbine

Currently talks are in progress between Bournemouth Council and the owners of Throop Mill to revitalise the building. Hopefully the deterioration that can be seen from the outside: slipped roof tiles, blocked guttering, missing drainage pipes and overgrown vegetation is only superficial and that the building can soon be restored and turned into a wonderful asset for riverside walkers.

Signs of Deterioration

Throop Mill from the River Stour

Bibliography

Holdenhurst, Mother of Bournemouth Kathleen Chilver
From Watermills to Waterworks at Christchurch G.M. Dear
The Smuggler No Gentleman Michael A. Hodges
Dorsets Industrial Heritage Peter Stanier
The Makers of Christchurch Michael Stannard